T0392318

The History of the Gborho people of Grand Gedeh, Liberia.

The history, traditions and culture of the Gborho people from the distant past down to present.

Henry Kohn Glay

To order additional copies of this book, contact:
Xlibris
844-714-8691
www.Xlibris.com
Orders@Xlibris.com

ISBN: Softcover   979-8-3694-1241-1
            EBook   979-8-3694-1432-3

Library of Congress Control Number: 2024900095

Print information available on the last page

Rev. date: 05/29/2024

CONTENTS

Dedication..v

Acknowedgements vii

Preface ix

Introduction xiii

Chapter 1   The Origins of Krahn People 1

Chapter 2   Gborho migration...3

Chapter 3   The Georgraphy of Gborho 8

Chapter 4   Gborho Quest For Education..10

Chapter 5   Gborbo Past Leaders 1910 - 2002 18

Chapter 6   Gborho Economic Resources 21

Chapter 7   Gborho Division 22

Chapter 8   Gborho ROLE models...24

Chapter 9   Gborho Cultural Heritage...33

Chapter 10   Gborho and Grebo Connections 38

Chapter 11   Tuzon Quarters History...40

Chapter 12   The synopsis of Wahoo Family 52

Chapter 13   The first Europeans to visit Gborho land. 60

Chapter 14   Life of Zoh Gborbo Glay 62

Chapter 15   History of my mother Frances Nyoncia Glay...................69

Chapter 16   History of my Stepmothers. 75

Chapter 17   Village life 78

Chapter 18   The 1980 Military Coup episode in Zwedru.....................81

Chapter 19   Mayeato, the Great Warrior 85

Chapter 20   Life struggle. 87

Chapter 21   The Game Changer 89

Chapter 22   The devastated blow..93

Chapter 23   Tuzon women. 95

DEDICATION

To the loving memory of my beloved Mother Frances Nyoncia Glay and my father Zoh Gborho Glay. To the elders and wise men of Gborho; to Mr. Norman R. Peters my first Peace Corps teacher; to My brothers and sisters who have encouraged me to write this short and informative history. To my wife and children for their patience during time of writing this book.

ACKNOWEDGEMENTS

I owe a great deal of gratitude and appreciation particularly to God and the Krahn people in general, especially the citizens of Tuzon and the God-fearing people of Gborho, for their love, compassion and humanitarian supports for my mother, which helped sustained her life. Many similarly captured children by the Liberian Frontier Force (LFF) soldiers from their homeland, during the Sassatown's war did not survive their first anniversary in their captive land.

To the Government and people of the United States of America, especially to President John F. Kennedy and Sargent Robert Shriver who envisioned the idea to form the Peace Corps program. This organization afforded me the opportunity to meet Mr. Norman R. Peters the first Peace Corps Volunteer assigned to the primary school in my area. Upon his arrival my dad embraced him wholeheartedly and claimed him as unofficial adopted son. In returned young peters at the time developed a keen interest in the educations of his children. Mr. Peters was instrumental for my brother Wilmot to attend Catholic schools, St. Patrick High School in Monrovia, Gonzaga Collage High School in Washington, DC and Providence College, Providence, Rhode Island. Mr. Peters helped to writes the transcript of the oral history of our area as told by my father and his uncle Old Man Chaarh Robert. The photographs in this book were made possible through the generosity of Mr. Peters who took them and preserved for many years. I will be forever grateful to him and America.

To my brother Hon William K. Glay and his wife Madam Naomi L. Glay for their sponsorship of my trip to America for school prior to Liberian rebels war. To my wife

Edith who helped with typing and proof reading of the manuscript. To my grandkids who were cooperative in the writing of this book with less interruptions. To the former Ambassador Harold G. Tarr, I considered a living encyclopedia for helping with the spelling of the Krahn words. To the renounced journalist comrade Kai G. Wleh for his encouragement in writing this book. To my brother Peter B. Glay who helped with some historical and cultural information. To my nephew Fortress Kohn Glay who helped with the Krahn words spelling versions in French and all those helped with information in writing this book. Thank God for the strength and courage in writing these accounts of history as was told and experienced.

PREFACE

Author: Henry K. Glay

Author: Henry K. Glay

Henry Kohn Glay thoughts to have become a traditional chief of his native land. To bring into reality repeated dreams of the wise men and respected elders of Gborho, Tuzon. The ninth (9th) of the 11 children of his mother. Who grew up in a tiny village, In Tuzon raised by many stepmothers alongside his biological mother and father, signified an Igbo proverb which says "Its take a whole village to raise a child" He lived and experienced life in a polygamy family, father of seven wives. He lived a typical disadvantage African child life experienced, with limited opportunities poverty striking environment. However, with the intervention of Mr. Norman R. Peters, Peace Corps volunteer teacher, encouraged his parents to send him to school instead teaching him oral history of the clan. He was considered metaphorically the walking stick (cane) and tape recorder of his father. He goes nearly everywhere with his father. He received his Elementary education from Zai town public school ZTPS an hour thirty minutes walking distance from his father village to the school after completed six grades, briefly enrolled at Tubman Wilson Institute, TWI. subsequently to Zwedru Multilateral High Shool (ZMHS) and received his college education from the Southeastern university, (SEU) Washington, DC . He obtained his undergraduate degree Bachelor of Science (Bsc) degree in Business management, and took graduate courses in Government management.

Henry Kohn Glay Librarian and educational Aide.

He briefly worked at the Liberian Embassy Washington, DC in the office of information and public affairs division. He worked with the DC Public School System as Librarian Aide and educational Aide, Substitute Teacher Howard County Public Schools system, International Monetary Funds (IMF) and National Institute of Health (NIH) security officer respectively, PG county Park and Recreation Potomac learning center Assistant Director.

Henry is an active member of the Southeastern university Business Administration Alumini Association of Washington DC, A community advocate and leader, served on the Union of Liberian Association in the Americas (ULAA) board representing Washington DC Metro. Chapter, member on ULAA Election commission, Chairman GGAA election Commission, President GGAA, DC metro. chapter and national president Grand Gedeh Association in the Americas, Inc (GGAA) He is a devoted catholic and member of the Knight of Columbus. Legally married to Edith Carr Glay and father of seven children, many grandchildren and two great granddaughters at the time of writing of this book, and many children.

Special Note: Krahn Names

In the Krahn culture people often use first name instead first and last name. But name which complements their parents name either the father and mother names or both. example my name Zoh Kohn or Nyoncia Kohn. Gborbo, Gbabo, Gorbo ect. are the current spellings and pronouncements of these words however traditionally these names were pronounced Gborho, Gbao, Gorho by Krahn people. The 'bo' was added to many Krahn names by the so-called Americo -Liberians through their Frontier Force soldiers made up especially of the Loma, Kpelle, Gio and Vai ethnic groups.

INTRODUCTION

The meaning of Gborho is "To gather, or to pull together " based on oral history and interviews includes personal experiences. This reflection is the result of many interviews with elders of Tuzon in collaboration with some manuscripts and journals written and conducted by Mr. Norman R. Peters former Peace Corps volunteer, Mr. Peter P. Nyanabo, the teacher of Tuzon tribal school and Wilmot T. Glay, student. In this book you will read accounts of the ordeals experienced by the Gborho people contributions and developments in the Liberian society. How things happened and their perpetrators. Pictures includes were taken in the 60s and 70s with the exception of Zoh Gborbo Glay picture of 1929 in the Liberian Frontier Force uniformed. I was encouraged to document what I am told, experienced and read. It is often said to preserve you must document in writing what is significant. Therefore, the intent of this reflection is the historical narrative primarily involving how Gborho people arrived at this point and the motivational factors which evolved the transformations of life, specifically to explain life history, as orally told by our forefathers passed on from generations to generations. The stories in this book include those personally experienced and passed on to us. I want the readers to know the origins of their neighbors, friends, coworkers, classmates and love ones.

The origins of Gborho people family linkages and relationships. The goal is to enlighten the minds of the reader, generations born and unborn, those whose bloodlines (DNA) runs through the Gborho land, to be knowledgeable of the past and from where they have come.

To be prepared as the torch been passed on to them as were done by generations before us and future generations. I decided to include the transformational process of our lives and how to preserve and maintain the history and legacy of our forefathers of Gborho people. Reader in this book you will view historical photographs of people, friends, you and of yours relatives. This is an opportunity to see people and family members you never saw, only heard of. The caption on each photograph will explain in this book entitle " The History of the Gborho people of Grand Gedeh County" We are reflecting and retrospection on the past deem necessary. The photos include were taken and preserved by Mr. Norman R, Peters peace Corps volunteer teacher assigned in the Gborho region, Zai Town Public School in 1966.

Life has stages, the past is not your destiny, don't be ashamed of your past, or photos that is history be proud of it. Making clear example of myself as a village boy and present photos speaks volume. Reader in this book I will also elaborate on the quarters of Tuzon.

My village life

CHAPTER 1

THE ORIGINS OF KRAHN PEOPLE

Before the name Krahn which derived from the mispronunciation and misspelled of oldman Krai name the leading elder of Klaon clan-when the Liberian government soldiers the Frontier Force penetrated into the territory across Cestro river the government people encountered Oldman Krai leading elder of Klaon tribal section. The government people asked them to identify themselves? In response "We are from Krai-bli (bli mean place), we are Krai-youn (youn mean people" Originally Krahn tribe is known as (WE) Wehu or wenyon meaning people that are sympathetic, easily forgiven. In the Ivory coast officially known as Guere, another version of Krahn meaning is those who made covenant with God so that God may bless them and redeem them in time of trouble. This is the attribute of Krahn Jewish heritage(Kaiser Memorial Lawn cemetery). Before delving into the short history of Gborho, we will firstly delve into the origins of Krahn tribe from the holistic perspective which Gborho is a subsection. We are orally told consistently that all Krahn tribal groups originated from Nyan-yah. Nyan-jah mean top of the hill or hill top. According to the stories told from time to times wars after wars, includes French invasion in 1894 that drove group of people out of the grassland into the rain forest. One group of these people were the Krahn Tribe who built a town on the top of a large maintain and named the town Nyanjah in the Northeastern part of modern-day Ivory Coast. However, no one seems to have identify where Nyanjah is particulary located. In Nyanjah God divided Krahn people into sections and quarters to distinguish their ascent and pronunciations, each with special laws (Taboos) and talents. Krahn ethnic group is divided into 42 sections between Ivory Coast and Liberia. In Ivory coast the Krahn ethnic group is referred to as Wee, Guere or Wobe. The Krahn of Liberia have two subgroups, the eastern krahn are approximately 86,500 and the western Krahn of Liberia is 106,000. In the Ivory coast krahn are 360,000. Between 1750-1760 Krahn ethnic group reached the cavalla river.

The 16 Liberia- Krahn sections are:

1. Niao 2. Gborho 3. Zelapounb 4. Konobo 5. Putu 6. Tchien 7. Kannah 8. Gorbo 9. Gbao 10. Gbarzon 11. Plo 12. Gbo 13. Mao 14. Gao 15.Ninju,16.Ninzao, Glio,Twabo

These mentioned above Liberian Krahn sections are divided into three (3) districts in Grand Gedeh county. Tchien, Konabo and Gbarzon.

1. **Tchien District:** Comprises of these sections: Tchien, Kannah, Godho, Nao, Gborho, Zelapoun.
2. **Gbarzon District:** Comprises of : Gbarzon, Gbao, Gao,Plo, Gbo, Ninju,Mao.
3. **Konabo district:** Comprises of these sections: Konabo, putu,Tuabo,Gleo

The 26 Ivory Coast- Krahn sections are:

1. Niao, 2. Gborho, 3. Zar, 4. Zebeyor-kuo, 5. Jao, 6. The Beao, 7. Beaou, 8. Tcheon-Gawo, 9. Chien, 10. Gblean, 11 Tchameson, 12. Soohan, 13. Zenyeah, 14. Nennyeo, 15. Flaco, 16. Dahou-Dehou, 17. Bleao, 18. Wleoin, 19. Zleon, 20. Zonheon, 21. Bawah, 22. Nejluo, 23. Beawah, 24. Wonbee, 25. Gao, 26. Zilapoun.

2
CHAPTER

GBORHO MIGRATION.

Gborho people lived in Nyanjah for hundreds of years. Nyanjah grew with many different sections and quarters of the Krahn tribes were established. Near Nyanjah there was a huge mountain that was sacred to the Gborho/Krahn in general. On that mountain lived an Oracle assumed to be a messenger from God (Yonsowah meaning older person as well as God in Krahn). God would send messages to the people through this oracle. Nyanjah became overly crowded with people of different sections and quarters that shares similar historical linguistic and cultural traits. Be aware that all Krahn dialects sound so much alike with slight variations in the pronunciations of words.

Between 1714-1910 in search for fertile land Gborho decided to leave Nyanyah and moved further into the rain forest towards the Sea Coast. Whenever a section or family of Nyanjah decide to leave, the elders of that family or section would go for consultation to the Oracle of the mountain and ask for advice. The Oracle would advise them about what to do and what not to do. Each section or quarter that left Nyanjah were also given a different dietary law (Taboo) by the Oracle about what to eat and forbidden to eat. The Gborho having left Nyanjah, moved slowly Southwest toward the sea coast. They would engage in a fight for land to settle, defeat the people, take their lands, and built new towns. This was repeated over and over always moving toward the Sea coast. The first large river Gborho section reached was River Zo where they built a large town. Later they crossed River Zo and built another town. Unsatisfied with the area the later moved on until they reached the Cavalla River (Present day boundary between Liberia and Ivory Coast) where they built towns on both side of the river. Today you will find most of the Gborho concentrated in the Ivory Coast where they occupy large area of land. Gborho built eleven (11) towns and villages in Ivory Coast. Those towns are spelled in French and as they are call in Krahn vernacular (dialect).

Ivorian - Gborho towns are:

1. Zuu-(Zou-Yahi) 2. Zuway-zohn(Petite Guiglo) 3. Zai-bli-Dedjean) 4 Juan-blii(Tuambli) 5. Karwojuzon-(Kouadekezon) 6. Tel-ooh-(Tinou) 7. Johbokin-(Diboke) 8. Sharblii-(Medibli) 9. Gbowooh-(Zilebli) 10. Layeetahe blii-(Oulaitaibli) 11. Banyea-(Keibli)

Liberian-Gborho Towns are:

TUZON 2. BARGBLOR TOWN 3. ZAI TOWN 4. GWIEN TOWN 5. SOWARKIN 6. CESWEAN

These towns are situated on the west of Cavalla River and occupy the land between Gbarbo aka Gbao people and on the east by Gorbo aka Godho people . Gborho comprises of two sections Blaoo-Tiabo and Gborho (Chatane or Wahoo-gbaa) people with two distinct accents. Having crossed Cavalla river each section moved into different directions. Blao-Tiabo moved on the west and the Chatane-Wahoo-gbaa people moved on the east.

The First Towns of Gborho in Liberia were Jo-nee-wien and Gowah-nee-wein. Jo-nee-wien or Jo-nee-wein settlement of Chatane (Tuzon people) came from to build Tuzon in the 1920s and Gowah-nee-wein the Blao -Tiabo came from to built their towns including Bargblor town during the administration of president Charles D. B. King.

In Gborho/Krahn culture towns and villages are named after specific individual,tree,hills, creeks and river and animals.

Tuzon—means under the tree, was built by the Wahoo brothers Chaarh Diahn and Barhquiah Diahn, joined by their cousins Gbawhoo from Gbai-kohn bli(bli- mean place) and Zuwahoo from Glazon. Tuzon town is consider a mosaic encompasses of three families the Gbawahoo, Wahoo and Zu Wahoo, while Saye-younnu included as subset that joined later. In Tuzon the families are inter-related by marriage or blood. Each family (quarter) is noted for certain expertise and contributions. Zuwahoo are known as cattle rancher and mask dancing. Gbawhoo are recognized by their craftsmanship and mask dancing. Wahoo are known and recognized as warriors and boldness. Furthermore, in Tuzon each quarter has warriors : Zuwahoo warrior is Quihee-juwor, Gbawhoo warriors are Barh-youn and Kraah. Although each quarter has their warriors but Wahoo warriors Diahn and Diahn were famous and powerful, both served as kings of the Gborho region concomitantly, after the death of Barhquiah Diahn succeeded by his brother Chaarh Diahn. Unlike other towns Tuzon has no elephant hunter, but a charismatic hunter named Nukar.

Originally Tuzon had approximately 150-200 huts. Due to political and economic reasons some family members decided to relocate from Tuzon old town to built towns near the future Zwedru- Monrovia highway in the 50s. Old man Robert head of Wahoo/Chaarh-dee family for politicalexpediency was the first to relocate to built Robert's town outskirt of Tuzon. 2. Charlie Kahn Gaye moved with his Gbawhoo/powone-dee family to built his town Kahn-bli.

Those moved for economic reason were Geoage Zeon, Gaye-mahn Juwar built houses on what is now Tuzon intersection. Taye and Joloka moved and built Dajahan. These families moved before the construction of the motor road the Monrovia Zwedru highway in the 60s.

However, after 1980 military coup M/sgt. Samuel K. Doe, head of state, chairman of the People Redemption Council (PRC) native of Tuzon, encouraged the families to return to Tuzon old town, because conditions precipitated for them to moved were no longer exist through his leadership. Old Tuzon became accessible to motor road, with some modern houses and electricity. Nevertheless, some individuals remain at the intersection of Tuzon and Monrovia highway. Other factors of migrations, especially in the Gborho region are death of the town owner or person town is name after, lies, accusations of witchcrafts and outbreak of sickness or diseases. Most of the Gborho/Krahn towns and villages are name after individual, tree, river, hill, creek and animal. With the exception of Bargblor town built and named after a noble man Gawohn Bargblor 1945 who later became chief of Gborho land, died 1962 in Zuujah, an immediate border town near the Cavalla river bank in Ivory coast. However, since his death in 1962 Bargblor's town still exist comprises of four (4) quarters Blao-Nyao and Sauwhoo-Gaio.

Gwien town, initially built and named after Layee-jay-gbelay a noble and handsome man. Until Charlie Zoelar Gwien emerged. Charlie Gwien once served as district interpreter of Juazon district, under commissioner Woods in Sinoe county upon his returned in Layee-jay-gbelay town he became to assert influenced of manipulations and subsequently succeeded in changing the town name to his name " Charlie Gwien town". Charlie Gwien elected chief 1957 he was a no-nonsense chief Gborho ever had for 11 consecutive years before been dismissed by President William V.S Tubman during his last visit in Grand Gedeh county November 1968 predicated upon insubordination complained filed against him by district commission Martin Benson of Gbarzon district.

Zai town, built by oldman Zai and his Flye-dee family. Due to forced labor, maltreatments constant harassment by the government soldiers and tax collectors he and his family were compelled to sought refuge in the Ivory Coast 1947 where he built another Zai town both towns named after him currently exist.

Sowakin, built between 1951-1952 from the initial stage Deh and Gbieor the two brothers with their (Tiabo) family were living in Bargblor town. Due to confusion Deh and Gbieor left and built their town Gorbouyea and later relocated to Tuzon and subsequently moved to Sowakin built by Sammy Garwo Zarwah Gbieor or Sammy Howard not related to President Daniel E. Howard.

In the African culture especially Krahn tradition is prestigious and honor for female to perform special tasks more importantly like cooking cow head dish during festival. In Tuzon each quarter has destinated lady specializes and responsible to cook cow head dish in a special way. Below are names of destinated women of each quarter that were responsible to perform the task cook in a special way and style.

The Wahoo family had two ladies responsible to perform the task. 1.Elder Layee-zu-aye's wife oldlady Pam-yuwor

2. Elder Garwo-belar's wife - Nyaa-bla-nanh prepared 17 cow heads dishes in her life time, which was record breaking.
3. Gbawhoo family- Elder Slanger's wife old lady Mahnled

When Tuzon was built in 1920s the first individuals to be born in Tuzon are: Diehe-yonly (Isaac Doe's mother), Moses Y. Diahn (Samson Diahn's brother), Johnny D. Gaye (Victor Gaye's father), and Johnny T. Gbeior (Zohn Gbieor's father).

The Liberian Frontier Force (LFF) soldiers built their camp in Gborho near the Cavalla River in Gbarbli and another barrack in Gbarzon. After a while these two barracks were relocated to Tchien aka Zwedru and established the fourth (4th) Infantry Battalion barrack, named Camp Wihsnant.

CHAPTER

THE GEORGRAPHY OF GBORHO

Gborho land is situated between the Gorbo or Gorho and Gbarbo or Gbao people, on the east of Konee aka Cratane creek near Logan village toward Zwedru. On the west Toua-nee Creek formed the western boundary between Gborho and Gbarbo or Gbao people. Tuzon is the oldest Gborbo town in Liberia, built in 1920s.

In the Gborho area there is a big rocky mountain called Vanyea near Gwiens Town. The recognized hills in Gborho are:

Tro-Zien-meaning red hill and Gbla-tro-meaning conjoined hill. Liberian-Gborho Geographically contains two known rivers which flows into Duweh-Dugba river. These rivers are Ces and Dro-doa rivers. Ces river is between Charlie Gaye town (Kahn_bli) and Brown village toward Zwedru and the Dro-doa river is located between Zai Town and Ferguson town toward Gwien Town.

Tro-zien (red hill) is located in the Bargblor Town area while Gbla-tro is located in Ceswien area near Cavalla River in the Northwest region of Gborbo land.

Gborbo is divided into four parts East, west, north and south. Chamentane on the east. Woaho on the west . Gbor-quaih on the north. Blawo-Tiabo on the south.

Gborho have two distinct sections that are identified by their ascents and pronunciations of words. The two sections are divided by Di-nee-weh creek near old Pynes Town. On the eastern side of Di-nee-weh Creek is occupied by Tuzon people call Chatane-meaning the three quarters territory or Wahoo-gbaar- The territory is call Wahoo-gbaa, because wahoo quarter is in the majority and first to settled in the area. The western side of Di-nee-weh Creek is occupied by Zayee Town, Bargblor Town, Gwien Town and Sowarkin. They are called Blawo-Tirbai Gbaar or Cha-yeann-gbaar-meaning four quarters territory.

Prominent family names mostly concentrated in Gborho by section.

1. Tuzon (Chatane section) Gbawoo, Wahoo and Zuwahoo: are : Doe, Glay, Diahn, Taye, Nebo, Slanger Blayee, Bohngawo, Robert, Johbo, Garwo,Kar, Gwien, Zeh. Pennue, Zeon, Joloka, Kahn,Wright-Layee, Tody, Shar, Gbeledah, Juwar, Dumahn, Nyanabo aka Nyawo, Kohn, Krubo, Joh-Joe, Dayway, Bloe, Krah, Saydee, Zeh, Tiah, Kayee, Wlhsnant, Gaye, Wahyee, Gwien,Wulu, Browne, Kuly, Jaryee, Blay, Bloe,

2. Chayean section: (Blawo, Tabawo, Saawho,Gawo) are: Bargblor, Collins, Gwien, Seo, Quiah, Baye, Grear, Gaye, Dahyee, Gee, Zayee, Layee, Kulah, Soo,Tarr, Karr, Galah, Cole, Gbieor, Sayee, Kwedeh, Krah aka Clark, Paih, Jones, Joh-Joe, Tujalah, Banyea, Julu, Chayee, Gbarwoo, Tenneh – Dennis, Mlihee, Gedea, Tarlue, Tody, Gbaye, Garh, Fiaho, Gbaeyah, Garley, Tajubu, Baye, Zio, Blokrah, Tiah, Zeh

Note:

Names Similarity does not suggest biological link, example Gaye, Gwien etc not related to the aforementioned names to either sections. Those with western/European names were imposed on them by their guardian's example instead Ceacumum- Wihsnant, Tarjubu-Collins, Fiaho-Jarry, Gbawaye- Browne.

CHAPTER

GBORHO QUEST FOR EDUCATION

In 1927 the Assembly of God (A.G) mission opened in Tchien aka Zwedru. In search for education the first group of Gborho students began to enroll in dove between 1940-1945 under the first Missionary Rev. Emmuel Janson, Missionary Rev. Gerald Morrison and Missionary Rev. Randall E. White respectively.

The first Gborho students enrolled at the A.G mission school were: Johnny Gaye, Susan Zaar, Moses B. Taye, Iren Taye, Francis Slanger, John Tody, John Friday Gbaledeh, Willie P. Nebo, George W. Gaye, James Wihsnant, Joe D. Tay, Edwin J. Taye, Isaac C. Williams, Gaye-Bardeo, Walther Jayee, and Tommy Fineboy.

However, prior to the opening of the A.G Mission, Benjamin B.W. Collins was the only Gborho person who could read and write that got his education from Cape Palmas, Maryland County. Gborho was the next to have a tribal school beside Tchien. The tribal school was operated by a Missionary in Bargblor town in 1935 and another school was opened in Tuzon 1938, but short lived. The teachers of these schools were: Benjamin W. Collins and John N. Joloka. In October 1963 Tuzon tribals school was established. The teacher was a sectional clerk at the time who saw the needs to solve the problem affecting the kids during the rainy season to crossed Geesar Creek near Tuzon.

Photo of some Tuzon students in the 70s. Today each Gborho town has a school building, while Zai Town public school has been upgraded and renamed Gborho Central High School.

In 1960 USAID built Zai Town Public School and opened the enrollment in 1963 with twenty-five (25) 2nd and 3rd grades studebts. The first group of students were those attended schools elsewhere, and the second group were children who alway wanted to go to school but had no means increased the enrollment to seventy five (75). ZTPS the only government public school in Gborho. Zai Town was selected because of its centralized location and it is on the main Monrovia – Zwedru highway.

The first teachers were; Harry P. Gbawood, and Thomas Tugbah, Principal. Principa Tugbah was later tramsfered at the result of the citizens complaint filed against him for the ill-treatments of a student, for punishing the student with fifty (50) leahes on his bare back and obstructing money from students. The Supervisor of Schools Mr. Cyrus S. Cooper had no alternative but to transferred Mr. Tugbeh and subsequently appointed Mr. Jack D. Jaddah principal in 1963. Teacher Thomas Kofa came in 1965 follow by teacher John Jabbah. In 1966 Norman R. Peters was the first Peace Corps teacher assigned at Zai Town Public school . When Mr. Peters got sick Mr. Roger Wilsle was sent as substitute. Thereafter the following Peace Corps were assigned in Gborho, ZTPS: Larry Winderbaum and Bob and Myna Stahman. The presence of the Peace Corps teachers was a great help and encouraged many Gborho children to go to school.

Mr. Larry Winderbaum, Mr. Norman R. Peters, bottom photo Bob and Myna Stahman

Meet the 1st students of Zai Town Public school 1966, (L) Gabriel G. Wright, (r) Nathaniel K. Glay and the Glays brothers (L) Alfred, William and Wilmot.

Alfred   William   Wilmot

Below are the initial students of ZTPS in the 60s. A majority were boys: Gabriel G. Wright, Nathaniel K. Gaye, Isaac Juwar, William Koon, Nelson Wright, Mary Saydee, Alice Cole, Iren Joe, Harry Gwien, Edward Gbarwood, Isaac Gbarwood, William Gaye, Amos Zeon, Moses Glay, Amose Jones, Isaac Doe, Annie Zeon, William K. Glay, Alfred T, Glay, Wilmot T, Glay, Sammy Wright, James Saydee, Amos Gaye, Lucy Gaye, David Samuel, Tommy Gwien. Samuel Doe, David Jaddah, James Jaddah, Isaac Jabbah, Doris Quiah, John Wallo, Mose Wright, Wilson Gaye, Harry Gee, Dorothy Glay, Josephine Padmore, John Charlie, Sarah Charlie, Gibson Jaddah and many more countless numbers of students. Photo of ZPTS students the 70s.

After the military coup of April 12, 1980 the following former Zai town public school (ZTPS) students were appointed and elected to top government positions were:

Samuel K. Doe, Head of State, Chairman of the People Redemption Council (PRC) and democratically elected President 1985, William K. Glay, Member House of Representative, Jackson E. Doe, Asst. Director, SSS. Washington W. Garley, Superintendent, GGCO. Col. Harrison T. Pennue, PRC member, Gen. Alfred T. Glay Aide-de-camp to the President, Gen. Moses Wright commander 1st Infantry Battalion, Col. Moses B. Glay, Sr. Aide to the head of state.

Gborho means of disseminating information by various methods of communications, before the modern information technology systems, like telephone, fax, telegrams, emails, text messengers.

Gborho people used to communicate through various means, beating of the special emergency drum, a very large drum called (Duwa Towu) mainly used to alert people in case of major events. Example: attacks by wild animals, loss of hunter or any other persons, declaration of war, death of warrior, a well-known person, an elderly person or any important event. Also, messages were sent by disciples of masks dancers - masquerades to carry important messages. In larger towns information was spread by the blowing of horns (Ghanwohn) of large animals. Some towns had destinated town crier who went around the town spreading the message to inform the citizens of unfolding developments. Another mean to send messages bye-passer traveling to the intended village or town. The method used were to tie a rope on the person wrest as bangle to remind the carrier to deliver the massage, the massage receiver will untired the bangle off the carrier wrist.

Tuzon school students 1975 with teacher Doe

Grand Gedeh County 1980 superintendent S/sgt. Washington Wellah Garley, flank on the (L) chief Harry Bull Nyonly and Chief Brown Z. Gaye

Mr.Larry Winderbaum, Peace Corps Volunteer Teacher.

Henry K. Glay and Norman R. Peters.

Mr and Mrs. Bob and Myna A.I. Stahman,Peace Corps Volunteer teachers

Col. Harrison T. Pennue, People Redemption Council (PRC) member played gallant role on April 12, 1980 military coup.

The Glay's brothers Maj. Gen. Alfred T. Glay, sr. assassinated April 25,2002 in Ghana Liberian refugee Camp. Hon. William K. Glay, sr. member Liberian House of Representative 1985-1990 and Col. Moses B. Glay, sr. senior aide to president Doe 1980-1990 killed by Prince Y. Johnson's INPFL rebel forces.

17

CHAPTER

GBORBO PAST LEADERS 1910 - 2002

During the days of old Gborho people had their leaders according to quarters, towns, clan and region that were called Blowah-johyee or Kon-blowah-meaning owner of the land with supreme authority, before the introduction of the western governing system. That changed their title from Kings to Chiefs, Clan chief and Paramount chief. The Gborho people had their traditional leadership styles. Their elders are responsible in the selection process of their leaders. Mostly leaders are selected based on a leadership traits either from the father or mother background or both . sometimes warriors and wise men are chosen as leaders. The elders had the supreme authority to decide who would be their leader. The criteria were very simple and clear for an individual to ascend to Gborho leadership, be outspoken, wise, brave, well respected, be a family-oriented person, always be in readiness to defense Gborho's interests, decent physical appearance well built with charisma. However, all those attributes cannot be found in an individual, most importantly be a person of good moral character, wise, outspoken and good appearance be a family man (married) even with many wives as you choose. The process was peaceful and unique. The elders and warriors would gather in the absent of the potential candidates and discussed each character thoroughly before the consensus was reached. The elders will invite the chosen person to explained the history of the clan or region culture including the past leaders' behaviors and styles in running the affairs of the clan and their expectations before the initiation ceremony.

However, the introduction of western form of governing system disrupted the cultural and traditional style of administrating the affairs of their land mostly the establishment of the electoral system. Which opened the Pandora box for anyone to seek leadership position irrespective of their parental background. The process of voting by secret ballets to present which Africans have not understood.

Note: Kon-blowah, Blowah-johee-meaning owner of the land or land owner. King title were giving to them by the British explorers, subsequently retitled as Chief, Clan and Paramount chiefs.

The Kon-blowah or Blowah-johyee or Kings of Gborho from 1921 to 1956 selected by the elders were: King Barhquiah Diahn, King Chaarh Diahn, King Tenty Zellay, King Writyee, King Mombli, and King Gahnwon Bargblor. Gborho chiefs elected between 1956-1978 through western style by head counts were Chief Charlie Gwien, Chief Charlie Kpasuah, Chief Solo Bloe, Chief Arthur J. Gaye, Chief Isaac K. Diahn. Chiefs mentioned above were elected by voters lining up in que behind candidate of their choice for head counts rather than secret ballet.

Traditional methods used to dispense justices. These are methods and methodology used by traditional people in investigations. To reach decision in cases they will apply the following methods to determine the truth by applying the methods call Sasaywood. Examples the used of liquid from the bark of certain tree (Gor) drop the liquid four times in the accursed eyes, being certain that the accused will be kept in an isolated place for an hour covered the accused head with white cloth. After an hour the individual will come out to removed the white cloth over the accused head. The accuser, the chief or elder council representatives will look in the eyes of the accused to determine whether the accused is guilty or not. To determine When the accused eyes turned red it means guilty but if the eyes are clear as normal as they were before dropping of the liquid in the accused eyes means not guilty.

The other methods is to drink what they called "Sasaywoo" by using a certain tree (Julu- tu) bark. The bark is placed in a bucket of water and the accused drink it, when the accused vomits or throw out the liquid meaning the accused is not guilty, but in the event the accused does not vomit or throw out and the stomach begin swollen up that is the sign of guilty which is dangerous. The elders are required to apply certain methods immediately to have the accused vomit the liquid else the accused will die instantly. Whenever there is rumors of accusation involving your name which you believed is untrust intended to tannish your reputation you could willingly drink the sasaywoo to vindicate yourself, without been accused for the elder or chief administrating it to you. Another method is by applying certain traditional chemical (herbs) on the accused leg and place a hot cutlass from the fire on the accused leg. When the accused jerks his leg or is scared and removed his leg or act brave to get burn and has blisters on his leg it mean guilty. A not guilty individual the cutlass will be cold when applied on his leg. The fourth technique ascertain truth from an accused person by sending the person in the attic of a house build fire underneath to smoke the accused for a confession.

CHAPTER

GBORHO ECONOMIC RESOURCES

We were told between 1940-1950 British pound/Shilling was the medium of exchange. The sources of Gborho economic were: Rice, Cassava, Kola nuts, Cattles, Arts and crafts, Clay pots, meat, fish, palm oil etc.

In 1941 in the Gborho area toward the Cavalla River a gold creek was discovered and also a discovery of a flat large rock cover few kilometers or miles alone the route toward the gold mining area, which has the potential to be used for rock crusher company. The town built by Deh and Gbieor families with their well-known son Garwo Zarwah aka Sammy Howard not related to president Daniel E. Howard named the town after the flat rock (Sowarkin) -meaning on top of the flat rock. Presently people are conducting Gold mining operation in the area camp name Bartedjan or Batedjan by Chinese and local people. Gborho has vast fertile land suitable for mechanize farming and logging, the rocky mountain call Mt. Ven-yea which has never been studied for economic value, and the noticeable hills Tro-zain and Gbla-tro. Forest for hunting and many creeks and rivers for cold-water fishing. The Gborho people are subsistence farmers of Rice, Cassava, Plantain, Eddoes and vegetables. In the last five years Gborho people has begun growing cash crops on a large scale such as cocoa, coffee, oil palms, rubber,and others. The major diet of Gborho people is rice, cassava and plantain. However, Cassava, yams, eddoes, plantains, potatoes are eaten occasionally during time of bereavements. While rice and palm butter soup is the major daily dish.

CHAPTER

GBORHO DIVISION

The Gborho region is divided into five parts: On the east are Chatane; on the west are Walwo; on the south are Blawo; on the north are Gbo-Quiah; in the center is Saye-yune. Despite those five parts Gborho is further divided into several sections of families or quarters. Although Gborho is considered a minority tribal group in Liberia due to cavalla river which divide the Gborbo people into two sections, the Liberian Gborho and the Ivorian Gborho. In Ivory Coast the Gborho tribal group is in the majority and covers a vast area of land. The biggest Gborho town is Diboken which has approximately over one thousand houses. While in Liberia Tuzon is the biggest and the oldest Gborho town. Deeping into the Gborho history a lady by named Zarwlee was mentioned. Zarwlee was a single unmarried lady in the Gborho region. She had a brother whose name was Gayro but real name was Gbara or Gbarm. Zarwlee left the Gborho region and traveled to the Marbo territory and got married and born some children. This is why Gborho people considered Marbos their sister children and considered Gayro or Gbarn children Gbarns-Gborho and the children of his sister are called Zarwlee-yonue meaning Zarwlee children. Gborho other brothers took different directions and called themselves Niao, that occupy the land between Tchien and Gorbo people near the Cavalla River on the east. Prior to that Gorbo people had their town near the Cavalla River between Gborho and Niao.

The story of the Cavalla River. Cavalla River flows through many sections of the Krahn region before emptying into the Atlantic Ocean in the Grebo territory, in Maryland county. Cavalla River was partitioned among the sections that lived at the riverbank to be used as crossing point.

Gborho and Gorbo boundary dispute in the 1960s during the district days, Commissioner Frank W. Smith 1962-1963 served as District Commissioner the issue of boundary arises. During side brushing of the trail and road from the boundary of Gborho and Gbao people toward Zwedru the Gorbo people raised the issue after passing of the motor road in 1963, the first time motor cars reached to the Eastern Province, Tchien District. Gorbo felt the Gborho people were encroaching into their territory. The case was transferred to President Tubman. In the interim Grand Gedeh was declared a county in 1964. President Tubman sent the case back to the county Superintendent Mr. Moses P. Harris, sr. Superintendent Harris ruled in favor of the Gborho people. The proceedings, which took place in Dejillah, a Gborho village in June 1966, finalized the issue of Gborho and Gorbo boundary case which made Cretane-aka Konee Creek near Logan's farm the official boundary between Gborho and Gorbo people.

The amalgamation attempts in the 1972 by President William R. Tolbert's government tried redistricting and the merging of clans and chiefdoms to reduce the numbers of chiefs and development purpose. At the result Gborbo, Niao and Tchien were combined as one Chiefdom.

As a result of the amalgamation there were not any new chiefs from the Gborho. The new chiefs were Chief Charlie Kpasowah (Tchien) and Chief Solo Bloe (Niao).

However, Chief Mombli, Niao individual chief for Gborho and Niao before the amalgamation policy was instituted. Gborho and Niao were the small ethnic groups in Liberia but in a majority in the Ivory Coast, always paired together as Gborho and Niao by intermarriages even before the marriage of President Samuel K. Doe (Gborho) and Nancy Bohn Doe (Niao).

GBORHO ROLE MODELS.

The Gborho road models, these individuals and others the like of T Kulah Jarry photo unavailable are cradle of Gborho civilizations these individuals selflessly and courageously embraced the yoke of hardships in Monrovia, to battle the odds to become who they are in education, to occupied governmental positions, military and paramilitary positions. They were the first hail from the Gborho land to obtained and occupied positions mentioned above, and have been inspirators to the generations after them. To date huge numbers of Gborho people are following their footsteps in all aspects of life,

their good examples have been emulated. They are laws maker, administrators, educators, military and paramilitary officers. We also when to recognize Gborho important achievements and contributions, be it for self-aggrandizements or public benefits need recognitions.

Before the inception of April 12, 1980 military coup de tate Gborho citizens have been playing important roles in the Liberian society from 1910-1980. The first Gborbo men to be enlisted in the Liberian Frontier Force (LFF) were: Charlie Kaine Gaye, Zoh Gborho Glay, Daniel Nyanwo Cole, Johnny Gboaa, Gaye Sowyane, Saydee Fineboy, Debi Yahn Gaye, Borbor Mleyee Jones, and Gaye Gweyan. Most of them served alone with my dad Zoe Gborho Glay during the Sasstown war under the command of Captain Watson detachment commander, Sassatown, Sinoe County detachment, Lt. Heard, battle field commander, and Lt. Passawe the executive officer of the detachment.

Photo: Zoh Gborho Glay
Liberian Frontier Force 1929-1945

Photo: M/sgt. Samuel K. Doe
Armed Forces of Liberia (AFL) 1969-1990.

Samuel K. Doe, born on May 6, 1950 in Tuzon, from the Zuwahoo quarter unto the union of Mathew Gboaye Doe and Anna Jaytay Doe, enlisted in the Armed Forces of Liberia 1969. On April 12, 1980 Master Sergeant Samuel K. Doe masterminded the first military coup in the history of Liberia after 133 years of settler's rule commonly known as Americo-Liberian, decedents of former freed slaves from North America soil. M/sgt.Samuel K. Doe and seventeen (17) none-commission officers topped the TWP government of President William R. Tolbert, Doe as head of state and Chairman of the people Redemption Council (PRC) 1980-1985, elected president 1985,assassinated on September 9, 1990 by the rebel forces of the Independent National Patriotic Force, (INPFL) headed by Prince Y. Johnson, now senator of Nimba county. President Doe first indigenous, Gborho person to become president of Liberia first to visit the white house and to be given military honored by the United States government. In Tuzon young Doe played for the mighty Iron Gate soccer team.

HON. EDWIN J. TAYE

WILLIAM

In the 60s Mr. Samson L. Diahn, Mr. Edwin J. Taye were the first Immigration officers. Mr. William K. Glay and Mr. T Gbaku Wright were the first Special security Service officers to be assigned at the Executive Mansion and Mr. William Diahn, 1st police officer, Col. Alfred B. Chayee, first to be enlisted in the Liberian National Coast Guard.

Rev. Moses B. Taye (AG Church) 1st Gborho man to be converted into Christianity

Col. Alfred Chayee, 1st Gborho male enlisted in the Liberian National Coast Guard Service 1960s

Zoh Gborho Glay 1st Gborho man enlisted in the Liberian Frontier Force 1929, rtd 1945

Sharon B. Browne, university of Liberia and Annie S. Zeon, Cuttington university Gborho females to broke the glass ceiling to graduate college in the 70s.

The first citizens of Gborho region to travel to the united states of America in the 60s and 70s for studies were: T Kudah Jarry, Wilmot T. Glay and William Diahn. In the 70s Sharone Browne and Annie Zeon were the first Gborho females to break the glass ceiling to graduate from college to obtained degrees, Sharon Browne, University of Liberia, Annie Zeon, Cuttington University of Liberia, Edmond Z. Bargblor was the first Gborho male to graduate from Cuttington university 1978.

While in the mining sector Mr. George L. Zeon was the first to discovered Gold mining creek . While in the 70s James C. Wihsnant and Peter C. Kai were the first to found large pieces of diamonds respectively. John G. Tody first to become motor vehicle driver in the 60s Mr. Philip Tuwo Gaye first to owned a motor vehicle in the 60s. Fleight Lieutenant Aaron D. Gaye first Gborho man to become Air force pilot in the 80s. Gborho first individuals who took military training in the US in the 70s and 80s were Sgt. Moses Wright, Sgt. Isaac Juwar and Sgt. Washington Garley respectively.

The Glay's brother Alfred, William/ Wilmot

Edmund Z. Bargblor, first grandson of Chief Ghanwohn Bargblor to graduate from college and to traveled to the US.

iam Diahn first Gborho male and grandson of
an Chaarh Diahn to graduate from high school
o joined Liberian National Police (LNP) CID
n, Bureau of Immigration and Nationalization
(BIN),concomitantly first to traveled to US
to graduate from college.

CHAPTER

GBORHO CULTURAL HERITAGE

In the days of old the Gborho tribe was considered powerful warriors. During those days Gborho people were smart and sophisticated fighters in using their weapons. They had so many warriors and some of those warriors are doing nothing since there is no more tribal wars. The warriors can only be recognized when wild animals attacked. Exampe leopard attacked villages to destroy cattle's as a result they would come out to demonstrates their bravery to counterattacked the leopard to killed for pepper soup. The old warriors could do wonderful things when they are ready to fight. Some of them believed in the supernature and magical powers while some believed they could fly like a bat. They claimed to had a juju (voodoo) medicine called "Pit-Zuu"(bat spirit) while some of them had other medicine which made them believe they are invisible when an enemy fired at them the gun wouldn't fire and he would walk up to the gunner and seized the gun from the attacker called (Kuly-Zuu). These voodoo, juju super nature powers made them to be brave in fighting wars.

Krahn Masquerades Festival

Gborho have many social clubs and masks dancers (masquerades) to perform at festivals and special occasions. Among the masquerades they have powerful and strange frightening face masquerades that nobody can look at their faces, because of the type of design of their faces including sharp pointed horns and eyes. These are names of few important ones:

1. The oldest amongst them in Tuzon are: Gwayee-galah, Duopy galah, Towah galah and Julu-galah
2. While in Bargblor Town are Gayee- galah and Mlan-kpahe-zan.
3. Zai town: Kyne-galah.
4. Gwien Town: Kekpa galah

The head of Gborho people masquerades Gblo-galah is in Ivory Coast in the town of Tinhou. Gborho elephants Hunters become a hunter especially big games hunters you need to be brave and skillful in hunting elephants, Hippopotamus, Leopards, and many more. Among the hunters there are superior skillful and mostly experience ones. oldman Barhshar was the big game leading hunter. After the death of Barhshar, he was succeeded by Tahou Gbehe who became the master hunter who became successful. He remained in the game until he got older and unable to go hunting anymore but became the trainer of young interested Gborho hunters. Those trained by him emulated him and became the best hunters like him. The master hunter Tahou Gbaboue lived in Kahou-johzon in Ivory Coast he died in 1963. He was succeeded by Gbehe-Tiah also living in Ivory Coast, Zai Town (Dejean).

Old man Zai the owner of the two Zai Towns in Liberia and Ivory coast . In 1947 he and his kinsmen ran away from the abuse of power, force labor from the corrupt government officials inhume treatments of tax collectors and the Liberian Frontier Force soldiers into Ivory Coast.

Liberian Gborho people have two skillful known big game hunters: 1. Blackman Wao Gbior, who lived in Sowakin and 2. Peter Chameio Clark who lived in Bargblor Town.

Gborho traditional folkfort singersL The lead singers of Gborho were Gayee-mowom-Ivory Coast, Quaweah-Liberia and Doua Marie aka Zorhyan Doua-Ivory Coast. The singing masquerades were Tor-plu gala-Liberia, and Gbayah gala-Ivory coast. Gborho social organizations (clubs) according to age category

Zanwuon- senior citizens club (65-up)

Gbazeon-adults club (45-60)

Blafiah- middle age adult club (30-45)

Gowaah- youth organization (20-30)

The supreme native doctor juju man is Kayee-Inai, Ivory coast. The known handsome man in Gborbo is Lyon Tiah (Zai Town, Ivory Coast) and the known beauty queen Liberian-Gborho woman is aunty Barhzeon Wehlo (Tuzon, Liberia).

In the Gborho/krahn culture tradition demand what could be considered compulsory marriage of a widow to her dead husband brother or someone in the family.

**(L) Isaac K. Doe and (R) Moses B. Glay playing
Xylophone in Tu zon 1966.**

Mrs. Betty D. Krubo, traditional chief zoeof Tuzon with sendi bush girls and assistants Duwah and Duwah.

The Gbo rho/Krahn's cultural festival Masquerades preserving, tradition and cultural heritage.

CHAPTER

GBORHO AND GREBO CONNECTIONS

Gborho became connected to the Grebo people in 1910 when some Gborho men traveled to Tarbou Region and crossed Cavalla River than settled among the Grebo people, between the Cavalla River and the Sasstown area. Those Gborho men never returned integrated themselves with the Grebo tribe. Nevertheless, these people know they are Gborho among the Grebo people. The two Gborho brothers who remained in the Grebo region were Zarwlee and Gaylow. The two brothers born lots of children however for whatever reasons their disagreements separated them each of them took different direction. Zarree or Zarlee's children moved across The Cavalla River and settled in the area between the Gborho and Bihie Chiefdom. Zarlee took their original name of Marbo. Gayro children traveled toward the south and crossed The Cavalla River and settled in the Gborho Chiefdom and took their original name of Gborho-Gayro. There after treaties were signed between the Gborho people and the Marbo people, that both Marbo and the Gborho people are Dodee, meaning brothers of the same mother. Here after they were not to share or to see one another's blood, they were forbidden to do any evil or harm to each other. The treaty went further to states for whatever reason Marbo person or Gborho person commits adultery with a Dodee wife, because of the covenant between them, it is needless to claimed any damages to preserve, uphold and honor the Dodee treaty. Anyone who knowingly violates the treaty will face the rift and consequences. If any Gborho person travels to Grebo land today they will recognize Gborho person in that region. Today they are call sea side Grebo or Coastal region Grebo, or our brethren.

In the years 1914-1918, World War I was at its height and people were travelling everywhere in search for safe heaven and food. People were dying from starvation.

The Gborho and Garbo people connection that give rise to the Dodee relationship between the Gborho and Garbo people exists up to today derived from the helped of the Gborho warriors.

The Garbo people had confusion over woman issue among their sections that upset the other Garbo section.

Duwayee the head of the Nee-julue section of Garbo people, daughter was married to the other section called Wa-nio. His daughter refused to return to her Wa-nio husband. Du-wayee said Ok, since indeed they also have my son's wife, I will not allow you to return. The Wa-nio people felt that was an affront and provocation they declared war on Du-wayee and his people. The war lasted for four days with no one winning. Du-wayee called Diahn to support, Diahn the fearless warrior went to Du-wayee aide they won the war. In appreciation Du-wayee give his daughter named Sarlee or Zarlee to Diahn for the victory. Diahn accepted the girl and gave her to his son Chaar. Chaarh also had a son name Diahn. Note in the Krahn culture and tradition parents mostly will name their children after their deads relatives and friends signifying loved for the individual.

CHAPTER

TUZON QUARTERS HISTORY

In many of the traditional African towns and villages are divided into quarters. These quarters comprises of large extended families mostly descendants of one man. Most quarters are many hundreds of years old and the history of each is carefully learned, from the original ancestor passed down to the present. There are three quarters in Tuzon, providing the historic origin of the Gborho people. I will delve into the three quarters of Tuzon: Wahoo, Gbahwoo, and Zuwahoo.

Zuwahoo quarter elders. This quarter was founded by Jay-ku-or-flah in the town of Nyan-jah. Many Gborho people have traveled to different places including the sea coast, some returned and talked about their experienced with the taste of sea salt, that could be taking from the sea. This is the reasons that the Zuwahoo people decided to leave Nyanjah on expedition toward the sea coast for adventures. Jakuorflah had two sons: Manyea Jla-gbaa and Kulay. Manyea Jlagbaa had one son Tawugee, Tawugee had three sons, Layee, Doh and Nio, Kulay had one son Geelo.

Zuwahoo families following the parental line back to Nyanjah:

1. A) Samuel K. Doe, former President of Liberia.
   B. Mathew G. Doe father of President Doe, DoB 1902.
   C) Layee (Lite)-Tawugee-Manyea Jlagbaa
   F) Jaykuorflah, founder of the Zuwahoo Quarter of Nyanjah.

Zuhawoo Elders: George L. Zeon, Philip Tuwo Gaye and Gayee mahn Juwor.

(top) Oldman Gaye Mahn aka Try best Juwar and Son Maxwell M. Juwar
(bottom) Gaye Mahn Juwar, of Zuwahoo quarter wives and children.

42

Maxwell M. Juwar and family in Ghana, Liberian Refugee camp Budunburam

2. **A) Retd. Gen.Moses S. Wright, AFL**
   B) Peter T. Wright, father of General Wright
   C) Layee (Lite) Kowu aka (Wright)-D. Kulay

   -Tuway-Geelo

   F) Jakuorflah founder of Zuwahoo Quarter of Nyanjah.

   Pictures of Quarter representation

   A) Peter Nyanabo one of the first educated Gborho man and an early teacher who struggled for years to educate his people.
   b. Nyenabo aka Nyawo
   c. Naho father is Doh aka Doe,Doh father is Tawugee, Tawugee father is Manyea Jlagbaa, Manyea Jlagbaa father is Jakuorflah founder of the Zuwahoo family.

Gbawoo family:

The Gbawoo family of Tuzon founded by Barkuah (Barwaar), son of Barkuah brother of Mayeato the father of Wahoo family. Barkuah the founder of the Gbawoo family had one son Bajuwah, who in turn had one son, Bartejar. Bartejar had three sons it is from these three sons that all Gbawoo quarter descends.

The following are the different Gbawoo families listed with the oldest father first. The paternal line back to Barkuah.

1.Maenimah the founder of the Gbawhoo quarter of Tuzon

Barkuah (Barwaah) father is Barjuwah father is Bartijar father is Nyenao father is Dwehyee father is Baryone father is Weyhe

Charlie Kahn-ponlusobu Gaye- 1890-1982 head of Gbawhoo quarter (powon-dee) family: Back row (L) Rebecca N. Kahn, daughter, Helen T. Diahn-granddaughter, and son Lincoln Sohnplayee Kahn, and sitting are Teioh, daughter, wives Teioh and Zuou head wife. Retired LFF 1929 and former chief of Gborho chiefdom.

Oldman Kahn and daughter, oldman Blay and oldman Wahyeejue

Col. Alfred Y. Zeh, PRC member & wife Lucy.

45

The Slanger's Brothers Edward and JD

Amos D. Clark, Cecelia Gaye, madam Chewayee Tiah, Harrison Yeazeon Tiah, Gonyon Tiah

Cecelia Gaye, Jai Gonyon Tiah, oldlady Zue,

Rtd. Col. Alfred Y. Zeh PRC member Republic of Liberia

1.Maenimah father is Barkuah (Barwaah) father is Barkuah father is Barjuwah father is Bartijar father is Nyanao father is Gbakohn

Slanger.

Moses Slanger father of

Edward,Dennis and JD Slanger former Maritime Commissioner, RL.

Maenimah The founder of the Gbawhoo quarter of Tuzon.

Barkuah -Bajuwah-Bartijar-Gbawaye-Nyenao-Gbaikohn

Layee-joh

T. Gbaku Wright, former deputy LPRC managing Director.

Wahoo Quarter's Family Members

Wahoo family comprises of great warriors, their leader Barwaar was born in Nyanjah. He has two sons Mayeato who founded the Wahoo quarter and Barwaah (Barkuah) who became the founder of Gbawoo quarter of Nyanjah and Tuzon. The Wahoo family left Nyanjah and encountered Zaar people in war drove Zaar off their land . Mayeato has two sons Zeaye and Jehlaya. Zeaye was born in Teahee five walking days east of river Zo on the land taken from the Zaar people. Zeaye had four sons: Diahn, Jehlaya, Blay-nyanpan and Layee.

Wahoo is the conglomerations of various household families with the same parental backgrounds common DNA from generations to generations.

Mayeato the founder of Wahoo had two sons. Zeaye and Zeelee. Zeaye had four sons Diahn, Jeleya, Blay-nyapen and Lieyee of these Jelaye had all girls, Bli-nyapan had two sons, Yeazeon and Barhpaar. Lieyee had one son Gwien-zogarwo, Diahn had three sons Barhquiah, Chiah and Gbaah. Chaar had one brother Barquiah and his sister Lee-garyea. Barquiah born Diahnzo, Toorh-gbuwo, Jalayaa, Garwo - beelar, Gayee_byea, Layeon-gbo-ayea, Layee-Zuaa, Diahn-Pauoo.

Zoh Gborho Glay sunrise 1894-sunset 1974

Zoh Gborho Glay sunrise 1894-sunset 1974

Barhquiah grandson Oldman Charue aka Charlue (Willie Sinoe Garwo).

Chaar's grandchildren (photo)

Zoh Gborho Glay (Barhzeon Zoh) 1894-1974

Wahoo patriots top (L) Samson L.Diahn, Edwin J. Taye
William K. Glay and William C. Diahn

Wahoo patriots top (L) Samson L. Diahn, Edwin J. Taye, William K. Glay and William C. Diahn

Chaarh's sons are Glay-Wahyee, Diahn-Zo-gbehee, Gaye-chawu, Teahe-zaar, and Robert and Girls children were Bonyea-Nyon, Diahn-yealue and Nyean-garyah.

Chaarh first son Glay-wahyee, had two children: my dad, Zoh Gborbo Glay, and his sister aunt Wehlo (the beauty queen)

Glay-wehyee's brother Diahn-Zogbeyee had nine (9) children, seven boys and two girls: Kohn-jue, Fore, Duwayee, Yonslo, Isaac Zartey Diahn, Samson, William, Sawyea and Celue.

The Robert's brothers(L) George and Joe Robert, Alfred (f-r) bottom photo with Alex Dayway and friend.

Diahn-zo-gbeyee's children, Chaarh's grand children.

Glay-wahyee, youngest brother and last son of their father Chaar, Robert had 8 children 7 boys and 1 girl. George Gbarzayee Robert, Willie Johklaa Robert, Joe Johjue Robert,

Alfred Zweh Robert, Moses Kaar Robert, Philip Bloe Robert, Thomas Teaha Robert and Saynii Robert.

Robert's children.

Chaar grand children. George Robert, Joe, Alfred and Philip

Oldman Chaarh Diahn great grand children Photo

Amos Glay and Family

Harry S. Kar and Amose Glay

CHAPTER

THE SYNOPSIS OF WAHOO FAMILY

The origins of Wahoo family and who they are. The Wahoo are traditional warriors comprises of two subgroups Gba-dy and Tyar-lor Wahoos descendants of Mayeato. When the family grown they expanded their territory built their houses beyond Gba creek, adding "dy" mean behind considering those family members across Gba creek, Gba-dy wahoo. While other family members on the other side of the Gba creek recognized for foods productions were named Tyar-lor. Tyar-mean eat, Lor-mean town. That is why they are call Tyar-lor Wahoo. Food productions or eating town Wahoo. Present patriarch of Wahoo family Rev. Moses B. Taye, Samson L.Diahn, Edwin J. Taye, William K. Glay.

My Mom and Dad
Mr/Mrs Zoh Gborho Glay

The Wahoo's family names in general.(Gbaa-dy and Tyar-lor) are: Glay-wahyee, Robert, Diahn-zo-gbayee, Yeazeon, Garwo-belar, Blayee-zakpa, Taye-Gbobla, Blojuwar, Lea-glaykpa, Tody, Dumahn, Gwien-zo-garwo, Jobokayee,Nebo-geedru, Krah-mown, Joloka, Shar, Diahnzo.

After the brief general overview of the Wahoo family. The following are different family trees of wahoo listing with the oldest father first.

1. Mayeato-Jalaya-Gaye-Kahn-Mowone-Blayee-Zakpa
   Col. Benson M. Blayee former Police Task Force commander (1980-1990).
2. Mayeato-Jalaya-Gaye-Kahn-Joloka-Gbao
   Col. Arthur B. Joloka former 4th infantrybattalion cpmmander, Camp Wihsnant, Grand Gedeh county.
3. Mayeato-Gaye-Bartai-Kahn-Sayon-Taye
   Hon.Edwin J. Taye former commissioner of Immigration RL.

Meet the Taye's sisters Kama, Comfort & Betty.

Gbaa-Dy Wahoo

Gbaa-dy- means behind Gbaa creek. Having left Nyan-Jah, Zeaye built Poohdee town he later moved to Barquiah-bli onward to Jomiwein finally to Tuzon. From the family tree you will know who is Zeaye.

The children of Chaarh are:

Glay-wehyee the first son of Chaar had two children Zoh and his sister Wehlo.

Glay-wehyee's brothers: are Diahn-Zogbeyee, Gayee-chalue, Teahe-Zaar, Robert, his sisters are: Bon-yea-nyon, Diahn-yealue and Nyanna-Garyah.

Diahn-zogbeyee had 9 children, 7 boys and 2 girls. The men are: Kohnjue, Forte, Duwayee, Isaac, Moses, Samson, William and the women are Ma Sawyea and Celue.

Chaarh's last son Lawbert aka Robert had 8 children 7 boys and a girl. The boys are: Kpazahee, Johklaa, Johjue,Zweh, Kah Bloo, Teah and daughter Saynii.

The Glay family of Tuzon are great grandchildren of oldman Chaarh. Glay could laterally mean farm, or a type of juju for protections adding wahyee means completion of mission but figuratively not a regular farm or juju but as means of his father throwing jabs at his peers that got married at the same time, been the first for his wife to be pregnant among his comrades and peers. His mother was Barh-sowah hail from the Seyunu family her father was a native doctor. Chaarh went to consult with the native doctor, where he met my father's grandma Bar-sowah, their union was blessed with four children all boys: Glay-wahyee, Teahee-Zaar, Gaychawu and Layeeyawulu.

(L) back row Dorothy Munuah Robert, Lucy Nyon Glay, Gahnwu Gaye, H Bigboyd Glay, Collette Barzheon Glay, Ellen B. Glay front row (L) Harrison JUmo Robert, Amos Dugba Diahn, Helena Layee Glay

A look at the Wahoo family tree:

William K. Glay and siblings father is Zoh Gborbo

Zoh Gborbo father is Glay-Wahyee,Glay-wahyee father is Chaarh, Chaarh father is Diahn,Diahn father is Zeaye, Zeaye father Is Mayeato, Mayeato father is Barhwaah.

Samson Diahn and siblings father is Diahzogbayee

Diahn-zo-gbayee father is Chaarh, Chaarh father is Diahn

Diahn father is Zeaye, Zeaye father is Mayeato,Mayeato father is Barhwaah.

Joe Robert and siblings father is Robert,Lawbert aka Robert father is Chaarh, Chaarh father is Diahn, Diahn father is Zeaye, Zeaye father is Mayeato, Mayeato father is Barhwaah.

Willie Nebo and siblings father is Nebo, Nebo father is Layee Su, Layee-su father is Diahn, Diahn father is Zeaye, Zeaye father is Mayeatu, Mayeatu father is Barhwaah.

Glay-wahyee had two children, my dad and his sister Wehlo. Aunty Wehlo never had children but we were told she was exceptionally a beauty queen. People would travel from far places to come see how beautiful she was. Unfortunately, she died young in the 50s. I did not get to see her but my older siblings saw her. Her admirers would walk miles and days to come see her to shower her with gifts. Their mother was Barhzeon. Barhzeon's father, Flye Boho, was a great warrior of the Welgbaha people. After the death of grandpa Glaywehyee, customarily the Krahn tradition demand Grandma had to choose one of grandpa brother. She remarried to her brother-in-law Diahn-zo-gbe-yee, the fearless warrior chief of the Gborho clan. Diahn-so-gbeyhee raised his nephew and niece Zoh and Wehlo impacted their lives immensely. Chief Diahn had one biological daughter Veore. Zoh and his sister Wehlo automatically and noticeably made him to have three children. Zoh was in his teens when his father died while his mother Barhzeon was pregnant with his sister Wehlo. Every aspects of Zoh's life was attributions of his uncle Chief Diahn-Zo-gbehee, the great warrior who raised him made him the man who he was.

Names of Wahoo's family members of Tuzon in general.

Glay, Robert, Diahn, Yeazeon, Garwo, Blayee, Taye, Blojuwar, Leaglaykpa, Tody, Dumahn, Gwiensogo, Jobokayee, Nebo, Krah-mown, Joloka, Shar.

General laws (taboos) of Wahoo Quarter Pumkin, Blackbuck deer (A brown deer with straight black line on the back) Wahoos are allergic to, believed when eaten in time of war will caused enemy to be victorious. since indeed the wahoo are descendants of warriors are strongly forbidden to be part of their diet. However, irrespective to the general taboo each family has specific dietary laws example my father family are prohibited from eating reptiles with fork tongues, Cassava snake and avoid stepping on cassava peeling bare footed. My father wives are prohibited from preparing any dish contain this specific bird a gray vulture in Krahn call "Kan-wu-wal". This bird served major purpose that I have personally experienced on numeral occasions. Whenever these birds appear in group in the tree near our yard making loud noise like jubilating (hank-han, hank-han) a sign of expected good news. On the contrary whenever they appear very calmed, with a pitiful sound very low sad tune definitely we should expect bad news, especially from dad mother's section. It is believed to be the massager between dad and his mother's people.

Oldman Shar-Willie Layee and family

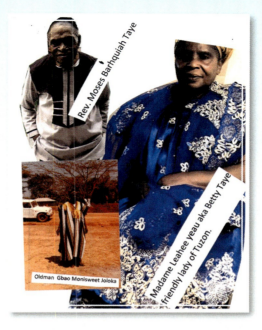

Rev. Moses Barhquiah Taye

Madame Leahee yeau aka Betty Taye friendly lady of Tuzon.

Oldman Gbao Monisweet Joloka

Standing (L) Betty Sa...
Poodeh Shar aka Shar...
Elizabeth Sawyea-nyo...

Mrs. Sarah Lee Diahn and Children, Margret, Dugba,Duoz...
Rebecca,sitting Anothny, Comfort.

Chief Isaac Z...

Ma Frances Dweh Togba and Children

Sarah Glaynyon Garwo

CHAPTER

THE FIRST EUROPEANS TO VISIT GBORHO LAND.

Around 1910 the first Europeans explorors the rubber traders arrived in the Gborho region . They traveled overland from Cape Palmas, Maryland county to Barhquiah-bli (town) which later renamed Pam-tro-jah meaning rich hill. This Rich hill name derived from trading of natural rubber latax for the exchanged of goods like salt, gun powder, cutlasses, utensils and texiles etc . The Europeans stationed at the banks of cavalla river where they built their warehouse. Prior to the arrival of the Europeans Gborho people had no salt, cutlass, clothes, and gunpowder. In exchanged to those modern items mentioned above. Our people would go into the forest in search for wild rubber trees to tap latex to sell to the white traders in exchanged for modern salt, clothes, cutlass, gun powder, brass kettles, etc. They were the first white people Gborho people had seen in their region. Around the same time the other white explorers settled in Ivory Coast, in the Gborho region in the town called Tuo-bli.

During those days women wore Bluweh to cover their body. Bluweh was made of the inner bark of a special tree. Men uses wild monkey skins to cover their body, they would cut down special tree to make Bohing- meaning wooden slappers footwear.

Our people are noted to improvise to make themselves comfortable. Whatever use today is the transformation from the past with improvements. During the period under review our people had no possible means to travel to the sea coast to get modern salt for their food, but they made their salt by burning certain tree into ashes, processed the ashes by putting ashes in clay pot with small holes for the water to drop into another pot to collect the ashes water. When the water begins to taste salty they will boil the salty water until it is dried into the form of salt. This salt produces good nutrients and taste for consumption. The name of the salt is zor-wu-tone or TuTone meaning tree salt. However, the construction of motor roads made traveling easy, which made the tradition methods of producing salt obsolete the thing of the past modern salt begin available.

LIFE OF ZOH GBORBO GLAY

Life of Zoh Gborho Glay 1929 Liberian Frontier Force soldier retired 1945. Sun raised 1894 and sunset 1974.

Zoh Gborbo Glay, born 1894 in Barquiah-bli his father is Glay-wehyee and mother is Barzeon. Zoh loss when her was teen raised by his uncle Chief Diahn. Enlisteded in the Liberian Frontier Force (LFF) 1929 and retired 1945. The Liberian Frontier Force was established 1908 by President Arthur J. Barclay, retitled 1965 as Liberian National Guard (LNG), In 1970 transitioned into Armed Forces of Liberia (AFL).

During Charles D.B. King's presidency, he called on the chiefs to bring youmg men to be enlisted into the Liberian Frontier Force. Chief Diahn took his young son Zoh, along with him to Kakata, presented him to the army recruiter. The recruiter took him on motorbike to Monrovia for training. The recruiter, instead of using his parent's last name, he used the Gborbo section he hailed as his last name Gborbo, that is how he became Zoh Gborbo. That was not limited to my dad many others found themselves in similar situation to be named after their tribe and sections, example like Saydee Gbarzon, Tarbo Tchien, Charlie Grebo, Charlie Gio, Willie Belle, David Niao etc. After training he was assigned with Captain Brewier, in 1931 he was deployed in Sasstown, Sinoe county, now Grand Kru county. In 1920-1944 during the administrations of Charles D. B. King and Edwin J, Baclay respectively the following Gborho men including dad were the first to be enlisted in the Liberian Frontier Force (LFF) were Charlie Kahn Gaye, Daniel Nyanwo Cole, Johnny Gboaa, Saydee Finboy, Gaye Sogwyane, Borbor Mlihe Jones, Gaye Gwyan and Debeyan Gaye.

Decuments found in his trunk preserved for many years states " Zoh Gborho DoB 1894 joined the Liberian Frontier 1929. Hailed from eastern province, Liberia" and by his own statement, he died at the age of 80 in Tuzon.

Zoh Gborbo Glay on duty at the old Executive mansion.

He was deployed during the Sasstown War where his first son Peter Borbor Glay was born 1935 in Fedorkre Town, Sasstown, now Grand Kru County. Peter followed his father footstep in 1965 enlisted in the Liberian National Guard and rose to the rank of Warrant officer retired 2002.

Life of Zoh Gborho Glay 1929 Liberian Frontier Force soldier retired 1945. Sun raised 1894 and sunset 1974.

The Glay's brothers,Peter,William, Henry, Daniel,& Alphonso

Col. Moses B. Glay, special aide to president Samuel K. Doe.

Maj. Gen. ALfred T. Glay, Sr. Aide de camp to President Samuel K. Doe of Liberia

Norman R. Peters family friend visit the Glays family Liberian Budunburan Refugee camp, Ghana.

Helena Layee Glay

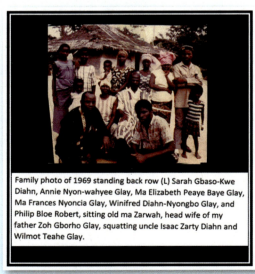

Family photo of 1969 standing back row (L) Sarah Gbaso-Kwe Diahn, Annie Nyon-wahyee Glay, Ma Elizabeth Peaye Baye Glay, Ma Frances Nyoncia Glay, Winifred Diahn-Nyongbo Glay, and Philip Bloe Robert, sitting old ma Zarwah, head wife of my father Zoh Gborho Glay, squatting uncle Isaac Zarty Diahn and Wilmot Teahe Glay.

Henry K. Glay

Henry K. Glay butching deer meat.

Henry K. Glay the bird hunter

CHAPTER 15

HISTORY OF MY MOTHER FRANCES NYONCIA GLAY

Frencies Nyoncia Glay, BOD 1927 in Sinoe County, of Sarpo-Kru parents. In 1937 the end of Sasstown war, war victims, captured children including Jah Nimely were brought to Monrovia by way of the Atlantic Ocean on gun boat by the soldiers. Among the captured was 7 years old Nyoncia who later grew and became her captive's wife. Upon their arrival in Monrovia she was taken to the eastern province, Tchien District #4, Tuzon in hammock. The hammock was the means of transportation to tote or carry government personals, wives and children in the hinterland before motor roads were built. Young Nyoncia growing up in the strange land who thouths her future husband was a father and head wife future mate was also her mother. Mostly in Krahn culture children are name after their mother or father depending which name is complementary to both names. Example my parents names are complementary to my name whichever way be it Zoh kohn or Nyoncia Kohn. In the case of young Nyoncia people thoughts her future husband was her father she was known as Zoh Nyoncia in the Gborho area.

We were told during the Kru revolt against the Americo-Liberian Government in 1931 the Liberian Frontier Force was sent to Sinoe county, particurly in Sassatown to stop the rebellion. One of the revolted chiefs were young Nyoncia's father, one of Juah Nimily lieutenants. Grandpa and other numbers of Kru chiefs were captured held in the army barrack. During roll called the soldiers were answering to their names little Nyoncia's mother heard the name Zoh Gborho after the roll called she bravely approached him, because Kru, Krahn and Sarpo belong to the Kwa group similarity in names, ascent and slightly different in pronunciations. She said your name appears to be of different orgin those of the other solders. Zoh Gborho answered I am a Krahn man and Grandma was surprised because most of the soldiers were of Loma, Vai and Kpella origins. Grandma narrated her story "I am here alone with our little daughter my husband is caught by the soldiers, assumed he is in the barrack. In exchanged for my husband release I will give our daughter " Nyoncia to help your wife she was between 7 or 10 years old at the time. Coindentally, my dad took little Nyoncia and turned her over to his head wife Zawah, who had given birth with her first son, to take care of young Nyoncia. When the war ended the army returned to Monrovia allegedly dad ensured grandpa Chief Mahlu-Vooryong was freed.

However, we read and have been told from other sources that 75 chiefs were captured and killed by the soldiers during the war. This doesn't suggest that grandpa was among the 75 chiefs killed or not the rest is history. The soldiers left on a Gunboat on the Atlantic ocean to Monrovia with some war victims including some kids especially girls. He took little Nyoncia with him they landed where the mansion is now. The area used to be the army base those days. From Monrovia they went overland being carried on people's heads in hammocks until they reach the eastern province, now Grand Gedeh County, Tuzon. Because my mother had no idea where she was and had no chance to escape. My dad played dual roles in her life as a father and later husband.

He raised her protected her and later made her his wife. Those days women were considered property. Their union was blessed with 11 children while six predeceased them I am 9 of the 11 children.

In the late 1960s some men claimed to be relatives of the Sassatown war victims especially girls children came to Tchien to look for their children captured by the soldiers, to complain to President Tubman at the traditional council sitting in Zwedru. The complainers states " Mr. President, during King and Barclay's administrations respectively, especially during the Kru War the soldiers killed our chiefs and took away our children mostly girls up till now we do not know their where-about of our children" Immediately the president asked the interpreter to announced in the council hall for ex-Frontier Force soldiers to be identified. My dad stood up in the council hall admitted, yes, Mr. President, I am one of those soldiers that brought a girl child with me. She is now a woman our union is blessed with 5 grown children. The security officers escorted dad and the people representatives to Tuzon to authenticate his claimed. Upon their returned to Zwedru that evening the security alone with the people representative report " yes indeed it truth" the people applauded. Tubman mandated the elders to sit with their in laws to amicably resolved the issue in interim pensioned my dad with $5.00 for his serviced and been a good man. Because other children similarly in the same situation died before the first anniversary in their captives land. Thereafter to re-establish connection with her people, to convince them that she is alive and well. Dad sent his head wife Zarwah and his nephew Moses Younslo Diahn to Sinoe to locate her family to reassured them she was alive. In 1969 my mother after many years went to Sinoe county to visit her people and stayed over a month until my father went after her and brought her back to Tuzon. Her children are William K. Glay, Sr, former member of the House Representatives of Liberia, Grand Gedeh County, the author Henry, Ellen and Ruth, their sister Koti few years ago joined our parents in heaven.

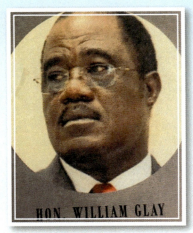

Hon. William K. Glay, sr.

My mother was resilience, disciplinarian lady, who endurance all odds. A teenager in an unknown land later became added wife to a man with six wives in a strange environment, under strange circumstances and survived it all including seeking for love, attentions and mates' rivalry. Let it be clear her husband protected her throughout before her death July 23, 1971.

Our mother Frances Nyoncia Glay

Ma Nyoncia's girls (l) Ruth, Ellen and Koti

Ma Nyoncia and sons William and Henry

HISTORY OF MY STEPMOTHERS.

My dad, an African who believed in polygamist lifestyle, had seven (7) wives with the total of 35 children alive and dead.

1. Old mom Zawah - his head wife, head wife status not by age it is earned for been first to married the man, it also comes with responsibilities and play a significant roles in the polygamy families, the confidant of the husband often time act as big sister, mother figure to the rest of the wives, and grandmother to their children. In the case of me and my siblings she also played duel vital roles in the capacity as grandmother and aunty, most importantly my mother's children that have no grandparents in the Gborho land, Grand Gedeh County in general. unlike our half-siblings whose mothers families and grandparents origins of Grand Gedeh County particularly, especially since indeed she raised our mother we thoughts she was her biological mother we considered our grandmother which she truly exhibited. Old mom Zarwaah hail from Blio-Tiabo section of Gborho, her father Kulah was a traditional folklore singer. During a festival my grandfather Glay-wahyee was very active as well as handsome, well-built with height. Old lady Zarwaah's mother Dukpa an admirer of grandpa (Glay-wahyee). She was pregnant with Zarwaah she promised grandpa that if the child in her stomach is a girl she will be your son's future wife. In their generations families will engage pregnant women in case the woman give birth to a girl child to be their sons

future wife. Fortunately, when she gave birth she had a girl Zawaah to honor her promised her parents messaged grandpa Glaywahee to informed him about the good news of his son future wife. In appreciation grandpa sent some items as token for advance bride price. As tradition demands when Zarwaah was of age to be married her parents, relatives and friends escorted her to her young future husband family's home for the marry ceremony. Both husband and wife were their first love and soulmates and for many decades. Their union was blessed with two sons, Peter and Kowooh. Kowooh predeceased them very early and survived by their son peter.

B. Layee-Zeyah, second wife was from Tuzon, Seyunu family, initially married to dad's cousin Gahn-Joh. When Joh died in accordance to tradition and custom demands, she should choose a relative of her late husband, she preferred dad who was in the army at time of his cousin death. The family sent for him, he came home and accepted to paid the bride price to her family. Their union was blessed with a boy and girl.

C. Gblo-nyonnon (Yaah)- from Tuzon, Zuwahoo family. When dad retired from the army he decided to tour Gborho region with his uncle oldman Robert, friends and relatives. They made a trip to Zai Town the home of his brother-in-law old man Kular Nyanoo-Daniel Cole also retired soldier, brother of his head wife Zarwaarh. Being young and handsome he was admired by many women and men. When the news surfaced about his date of visit a feast was organized by his wife's family and friends. When he and his entourage arrived majority of the married and single ladies began to sing traditional folklore songs in his name and honor the ladies flirting attitudes and behavior towards him made their husbands and boyfriends jealous to the extent that some men turned into violent against their wives and girlfriends. One of those individuals that disrespected their wives was Oldman Zarr Gee violently assaulted Gblornyon-Yaah to the extent that she was compelled to divorce him and ask that she married the man for which she was disrespected. My dad's uncle, Chaarh Robert, colleague of Zarr Gee, considered Gee action disrespectful to the Tuzon people especially Zuwahoo family. Being upset, the Zuwahoo ask that the Wahoo refund Gee's bride price immediately. A day later the dairy was refunded and Gblornyonn-Yaah became the wife of Zoh Gborho . Their union was blessed with four children two boys and two girls She predeceased her husband in 1965.

D. Peayea- from Bargblor town, cousin to old lady Zarwaah. When Zarwaah realized that after many attempts of her giving birth to a second child had failed she decided to return to her family in Bargblor Town to share with them her pain. Her family in returned decided to send Peaaye, a younger cousin of Zarwaah to marry her husband. The family convinced that she has potential of having kids since she was very young that her future children will become Zarwaah son's brothers and sisters. Zarwaah was overly proud to return to her husband with the important news. A week later Peaaye's family and friends brought her over to her future husband family where the traditional married ceremony were held and dowry was paid they became husband and wife. Their union was blessed with seven children four boys and three girls. She was the only surviving wife of my dad seven wives until 2022 when she passed away to joined her husband and mates with the lord.

E. Poein-daybo: A Tchien lady from Jabbah's town who dad met while he was in the military and their union was blessed with a girl.

F. Dallah -Tchien lady from Jabbah Town dad also met her while he was serving in the military. She was a sister to Poein-daybo when she realized her sister was in love with her husband she decided to leave and allowed her sister to stay with him. Their union was blessed with a girl child.

G. Nyoncia- from Sinoe county, who later became her captive wife, their union was blessed with 5 children 2 boys and 3 girls.

CHAPTER

VILLAGE LIFE

In an African society, children village life had lots in common. The villages are built in similar forms huts are built in circle with space in the middle for activities especially for children to play at night under moonlight. As a child I loved fishing, bird hunting and finding walnuts during farming season I helped served water to my father and brothers as needed on the farm while brushing. I did not engage in violent activities such as wrestling game, birds and rat traps settings but enjoyed listening to stories told by older folks. A fearless outspoken very vocal child, I would confront anyone irrespective of their age, status or relationship. People were afraid to gossip or talked about people around me. Example an elderly lady was talked about of being a witch in the town. One day I joined my peers to play behind her house we played for couple of hours. Often times my friends would go to her house to get water to drink. She realized we were hungry so she cooked Fennel rice as it is called in Liberian (koloqua) pageant English but actually is broken rice. She offered us, "children you all come and eat something". My friends ran to her to get the food. If she knew what in store for her, she wouldn't have inquired why I do not want to join my friends to eat? I bluntly told her that I learned you are a witch and I am not allowed to eat or to even drink water from your house. She was astonished and furious. Growing up people would be afraid to discuss others around me in their absent. My belief is "What you cannot say before the person don't say it behind them". Born radical and outspoken! Never smoke regular cigarette or take

in illegal substances. I was not allowed to drink alcohol. However I would occasionally drink a glass of wine or a bottle of beer not hard liquor.

Oldman Chaarh great grand kids. (l) Dorothy Munuan Robert, Lucy Nyon Glay, Gahnwohn, Henry Glay, Munnyon Collette Glay Duozon Diahn, Daniel Zarkpa Glay, Jumo Robert, Dugba Diahn, Helena Layee Glay and Ellen Chaa-Jaydeh Glay.

Tuzon 1966 oldman Shar aka Willie Layee. Barhquiah grandson.

Although we belong to the tribal group called Krahn in general a Gborho section, Wahoo quarter in particular this family primarily resides in Tuzon along with their cousins Gbawho and Zuwaho Quarters. The quarters inter-related either by blood and marriage an innate quarter where if you touch one you touch all.

Sporting activities of Tuzon. Tuzon has two soccer teams Mighty Iron Gate and Electric team. Iron Gate is consider the senior team and the Electric the junior team. Meet the Iron gate team of 1966 . Iron Gate was the champion team in the Gborho region and its archrivals were the Lion team of Bargblor Town, Mighty old Chapenzee of Zai Town, Straight Arrow of Tojallah's town and Mighty Old Zebra of Zleh Town. Iron Gate of Tuzon soccer team was undefeatable champion team the title held between 1966-1975.

THE 1980 MILITARY COUP EPISODE IN ZWEDRU.

The aftermath of the 1980 Military coup in Zwedru city, Grand Gedeh County. Although the coup took placed in Monrovia,but the army in Zwedru decided roundup, arrest government officials.

On the morning of April 12, 1980 Mr. Samson L. Diahn, county Projects Planner had returned from Monrovia with the county supplies. With no clue about the coup, even though he told us prior to his departure to Zwedru he met Doe on Camp Johnson Road. Doe had invited him to the Barrack (BTC) for his wife Nancy to prepare something to eat. He replied thanks but next time as he had already loaded his car with the county's supplies. "Oldman why don't you wait for tomorrow," Doe insisted, he stood his ground refusing Doe's offered. He said he noticed something strange about Doe's behavior, Doe stood still looking at him while he crossed the street going toward Internal Affairs Ministry. Uncle Samson, indicated he thought perhaps Doe might have had confusion with his wife that he wanted him to intervene as an elder who also his wife in law or really wanted to be generous or might have contemplated to hint him about what was in the making. Upon his arrival in Zwedru the early morning of April 12th I heard loud knocked at our door by military men. I opened the door halfway but pushed wide opened asking with authoritative voice where is your father, pointed their rifles at me.

Uncle samson came outside asked what happened demanded for his car key, hurrly, pushed him in the back of his own pickup truck with only his bed room slapper and tee-shirt on drove him away.

M/SGT. Samuel K. Doe, early days of the military coup April 1980.
Doe was born on May 6, 1950 in Tuzon, Grand Gedeh country
and enlisted into the Armed Forces of Luberia 1969.

With my traditional orientation prepared to be fearless no matter the circumstances. I asked where are you taking him? To the army barrack the army sergeant replied. What did he do? One of the army men replied we are arresting all True Whig Party (TWP) officials. Why, I asked? The sergeant replied with authoritative tone of voice, "They are no more in power." We were shock. As the oldest boy in the house Mrs. Diahn asked me to go check on the fate of my uncle in the Barrack. I consented while on my way to the Barrack noticed all streets were deserted with the exception of the army vehicles parading the streets shooting in the air vicariously arrested nearly all government officials including Superintendent John P. Beh, Col. Keita police detachment commander, Rep. Harper Baily, Samson L.K. Diahn county project planner and many others. The army took complete controlled of the city. While I walked by way of the radio station an employee of the station, Old man Sammy Sobah, had received called from Jackson Doe from the mansion who asked Mr. Sobah if he knew any Gborho person the section of Krahn he hail? I believe so the old man said. The old man knew was my father Zoh Gborho. When he saw me walked by he yelled Zoh Gborho's son. I looked in his direction, he yelled come, my son. I walked to him, he ushered me in his office, he asked to pick up the phone on his desk. I did, at the other end was Jackson E. Doe's voice. "Hello", I asked, who is this? He replied; I am Jackson E. Doe didn't you recognized my voice? Who is this I am speaking with? That is me I replied. Me who? Bigboy Glay I replied the name I am popularly call. Jackson replied Glaywhee, my grandpa's name mostly called in Krahn by friends and peers I answered yes. He said Kwety, the native name of Samuel Doe native of Tuzon he is now the President, I am calling from the mansion. Taffen, the native name of Harrison Pennue just killed Tolbert this morning.

In disbelief and panic mood. I asked, killed who? He replied Tolbert. Go and tell our people in Tuzon. I quietly dropped the phone in disbelief. I walked quietly out of the office passed by the old man. He called me back to ask, son what happened, what did you hear? I reluctantly told old man Sobah, that Kwiety and Taffen had just killed president Tolbert this morning, the caller called from the executive mansion Samuel Doe is the President. He was calling from the fourth floor of the executive mansion. I should go tell our people in Tuzon, in a very calm voice Mr. Sobah said my son, I know your father Zoh Gborho he was a good man. I strongly advice don't repeat this news to anybody as it is unbelievable. I left but without knowing what might happen I decided to go to Tuzon. Upon my arrival in Tuzon the town was almost like ghost town people were going toward the Liberia and Ivory Coast borderross the border. People were relief after an announcement which says: "I, Master Sergeant Samuel Kanyan. Doe, take this office because of rampant corruptions, misused of public office." The Tuzon people were not convinced because the Doe name was not a household name among the Krahn people unlike among Kru tribal group until Edwin J. Taye native of Tuzon was named Commissioner of Immigration and was called repeatedly to report to The Executive Mansion. We knew Samuel K. Doe middle initial to be Kweity from his father side. While his mother side Konabo knew him as Kanyon, which was not known by the Gborho people. With the radio announcement calling him Master Sergeant Samuel Kanyon Doe, doubt was created about his origin during the early hours of the coup. To make matter worse the popular lady in Zwedru, Madame Mary Gbah, alleged to know Doe to be of Kru origin that staged the coup. Later it became clear that it was Samuel K. Doe, a Krahn from a tiny village Tuzon.

CIC. Samuel Kanyon Doe, president 1980-1990 first indigenous president of Liberia. masterminded April 12, 1980 military coup which ended 133 years ruled of True Whig Party government. Captured September 9, 1990 at the Economic Community of West African States Monitoring Group (ECOMOG) Freeport base, subsequently assistant by Prince Y. Johnson, INPFL rebel at his Caldwell based.

MAYEATO, THE GREAT WARRIOR

Mayeato, the great warrior founder of Wahoo family in Tuzon,Gborho region. Who encountered great warriors he defeated. The greatest of all warriors was Gayla-podii-ar-sleo the great warrior of Fleo-Gaho region. Mayeato related to the Garho people on his mother side. In the days of our forefather's wars were mostly about woman and land issues. The war between Garho people and Zeylah-poun was based on woman issue.

The daughter of Garho family was forcibly taken by Zeyla poun. The action of Garho people considered as challenge and provocation angry them and decided to fight the Zeyla-poun people. During the war Zeyla-poun were stronger than Garho people. An elderly man said, "Oh we have our nephew Mayeato the great warrior of Gborho to come to our aide. Why don't we call him to help fight our enemies, we are loosen in this battle we have lost many fighters." Mayeato was called upon to help when he received the message regarding the war his mother people the Garho people need his help he consented. Mayeato joined the Garho people to fight, the fought for four days. The great powerful warrior Gaylar-Pou-dii -or- Sleo too strong to conquer. He has supernatural powers, lots of charms, he could appear and disappears. On the fourth day Mayeato caught a lady, he asked who are you? She replied I am the wife of Garla pou-di- or-Sleo, the great warrior of our land. Mayeato said to the woman, "Wow, I am going to kill you under one condition I wouldn't, if you are truly who you preferred to be the wife of Gayla-po-dii -rr- sloe the great warrior of the land. Tell me about your husband, including his juju, charms he has that made him powerful and difficult to conquer, else I will kill you. The woman pleaded with Mayeato please do not kill me. Firstly, I want to ask you, if you kill my husband the great warrior Gayla-Po-dii-rr- Sleo of the land will you marry me? Mayeato replied oh yes, you will be my wife.

The woman directed Mayeato where her husband was hiding. Gayla- po- dii- rr- Sleo has magical and supernatural powers, he would transformed, camouflets himself into young baby other objects and things. She directed Mayeato where to find her husband go in the bush near the town, look in the hole of a big log laying in the formed of young baby that is him. When you kill the young baby then he will be powerless and conquer. Mayeato followed the woman instructions after the death of the young baby, Gayla-po-dii-rr Sleo became powerless, weak and was killed. Unfortunately, Mayeato killed the woman at last.

After the death Gayla-po-dii-rr-sleo the remnants of the Zeyla-poun people surrendered to the Gar-or- people who then took over the Zeyla-poun towns. The Zeyl-poun ran away and settled in different part of the land. After the war ended, the Gar-o people gave Mayeatu two women to thank him for killing Sleo.

CHAPTER 20

LIFE STRUGGLE.

How far we have come to be where we are today. Many decades ago, I begin my life struggle in a tiny village with few mud huts, no pipes- bond water, no electricity, and no schools. The nearest school was hour thirty minutes away to and from. Because of the distance I started school at the age between 12-15.

In most of the Krahn culture children are named after their dead loved ones. The myth is their dead will be reincarnated to complete unfinished tasks. In May 1947 the voice and charismatic leader, no nonsense personality Kohn-jue whom I am named after died. Coincidentally the same time solar eclipse (when the moon passes between the Earth and Sun) occurred which further convinced the family that he was destined to be greater assumed to be the signed from God. His death delivered a devastated blow to the family. Ofcourse before I was born many years after his death. Many family children born before me were named after him. When my mother conceived many years after his death an elderly man, well respected, dreamed which he narrated that the my "pregnancy mother was my father's cousin Kohnjue. He said t Kohnjue was coming back to complete his uncompleted tasks in forfillment my parent need to perform special rituals to welcome him back" Immediately when my mother gave birth to me the required rituals were performed. A special taboo was given my mother to protect me. Few years later at age five the traditional training began to bring their dreams into reality. My dad would carry me to the homes of wise men and brave warriors in the region. We would travel miles and days to meet some wise elders and traditional zoes to witnessed some rituals been performed.

My Village Life

I would sit among old folks to experienced how to discuss and resolved murder, rape, devoice and land dispute cases. I witnessed elders applied wisdoms in resolving cases using logical parables and quotations to convienced parties involved, applying ordeals to bring the accuser to compliance or to say the truth.

21

CHAPTER

THE GAME CHANGER

Mr. Norman R. Peters, Peace Corps volunteer considered game changer, transformationalist embarked on the transformation journey of my life, after careful observation of my activities. He convinced my father to abandon the traditional preparation to become future chief of Gborho region, the wishful inclination of my uncle Kohn, instead to go to

school. With the acquiescent of my mother, the traditional preparation became history of the past. I started school in Zai Town Public School reading primer one between age ten and twelve, walking one hour thirty minutes to and from the school was tedious, at times experienced swollen feet. Mr. Peters was a great help, he helped to mold my minds which shaped the new course of directions of my life. When I completed elementary school, I left school due to the death of my mother July 1971. I struggled with the death agony and pain of my mother. I could not move with my elder brother William at the police academy Special Security Service training in Monrovia. My older sister Koti attempted to take me to her marital home in Ivory Coast in the village named Juan-bli or Tuanbli. However, Krahn culture forbids in-laws to live with in-laws, especially male child. Within the course of the dilemma and agony of my mother death another stressful tragedy hit the family, very unbearable one. On February 8, 1974 my father passed away left me with stepmothers and family members to care for me. Radical, outspoken fearless, spoiled by fatherly love it was difficult to be accepted by family members. My late brother Wilmot would writes through the Peace Corps to console me. In 1975 Wilmot came to Liberia to visit which give me hope in life but that was short lived. Unfortunately, upon his return to the states Wilmot was diagnosed with Aplastic Anemia, a rare condition in which the body stops producing enough new blood cells. Wilmot did not survive, he died on October 12, 1975. His body was returned to Tuzon, Liberia, for burial. That seem as dejavu, life became hopeless. However, William had already graduated and was working as Special Security Service agent assigned at the Executive Mansion, once again give me hope that all was not lost. In the process of these difficult years, I have a friend who shared similar situation with me. Alphonso Bargblor, whose mother died when he was very young, his sister Betty Nyongbiaye Bargblor was married to my uncle George Kpazayee Robert, he became my close friend, even up to today. He made me to befriend boys and girls from his area, Bargblor Town, Zai Town and the surrounding villages, the like of Sam Joe, William Baye, Alfred Layee, Mineva Bargblor, J Y Zio, T Zeh, Susue Williams, Helena Nelson, zarkpa Seo and many others. Through his friendship, I also came in contact with Rev. T. Kulah Jarry in 1976, after his retirement from Konola Mission where he served as principal. He collected us young boys and girls of school going age in our area, to returned to Zai Town Public School where he provided teaching. He later became assistant supervisor, assistant Superintendent for development respectively and concomitantly appointed superintendent of Grand Gedeh county.

In 1977 I literally forced myself on Uncle Samson L. Diahn. One evening he drove to Tuzon with his open back pickup truck, I jumped in the back of the pickup truck. Having no clue of my intentioned, I think he thought he was given me ride unknowingly he was taking a prominent uninvited guest to his house an hour later. His wife Sarah asked where was I stopping? I answered here, my uncle cannot have a house in Zwedru to search for place to stop or live. Aunty Sarah, asked did you discuss that with him? I replied no. She waited on her husband to return home, when came home. What was discussed between them I do not know. I only heard young men go in the boy's room to sleep. In the room I met aunty Sarah's two brothers, Victor Sleh aka Gaye Sleh and Arthur Sleh. The rest is history. I became the love boy in the home. I enrolled at the Zwedru Multilateral High school in 1978 and moved to Monrovia 1982. On September 9, 1987 after 8 hours long flight I finally we landed safely at the J. F. Kennedy Airport, New York City, where I was immediately directed to LaGuardia Airport for Washington, DC. I was met on arrival by my brothers Alphonso, Daniel and Annette LaBlance an Ethiopian-American lady, who had two boys with white DC police officer Ralph LeBlance. A very nice man he allowed my siblings Daniel, Alphonso and me to live with his children's mother at her 9th Street, NW DC residence. Every weekend he would invite us to his Fairfax, Virginia, home along with his sons Darin and Aaran, both attended the same school with my brother Alphonso. While attended Southeastern University. With the helped of Sharone Browne and Krayon Weefur, both employees at the Liberian Embassy, I found an apartment at 6645 Georgia Ave, apt # 207, Northwest DC. The first car I ever owned in America was a car note I overtook from Edmund Bargblor who moved back to Liberia.

Been ignorant of the system, the car was repossessed which I thought was stolen. I was without car for months and purchased a $500.00 used car from Morris Nyaway who also moved back to Liberia. My first job was at Marie H. Reed elementary school as teacher's aide and Liberian assistant. The important of credit in America, after I built up my credit enable me to secured car loan for the 320 LE Lexus. I begin Liberian Embassy local staff employee in the public affairs section during the ambassadorship of Eugenia Worthsworth Steveson. During the height of the oppositions politicians propaganda against President Samuel K. Doe an unknown person or persons believed to be against the regime of President Samuel K. Doe set the embassy ablaze and burned it down completely. I begin actively involved in the DC Liberian community, rose to the positions of ULAA Board member, Vice President and presidential candidates respectively.

My involvement in the community and ULAA politics allowed me to experienced the hypocrisies and sycophancies behaviors of some Liberians. The lesion well learned

CHAPTER

22

THE DEVASTATED BLOW.

Wilmot T. Glay, sunrise 1953-sunset 1975.

SPECIAL DEDICATION TO MY BROTHER

Wilmot T. Glay 1953-1975 recognized at early age during his elementary school days for his seriousness in learning Mr. Norman R. Peters Peace Corps volunteer teacher at Zia Town Public School developed interest helping him pursued for education Mr. Peter was instruments for his schooling from Tuzon, Grand Gedeh county, Liberia, Washington DC and Providence Rhode Island. WTG popularly called by friends and peers, death stocked heavy blow on the family, the Gborho region and Liberia. He was A+ student throughout his academic sojourned from Zai town public school, St. Patrick Catholic high school in Monrovia, Gonzaga college high school in Washington DC to Providence College, providence, Rhode Island. He earned himself scholarships included Martin Luther King, Jr. scholarship for academic excellent from Gonzaga Collage high school onward to Providence College. He was diagnosed with aplastic anemia a rare disease caused the body to cease producing vital bone marrow, on October 12, 1975 he succumbed to death. Wilmot was an athlete he played on his college soccer team. In his honor Providence College, name its soccer field Wilmot T. Glay's soccer field.

Wilmot Glay, 1953 - 1975

Pan American flight #182, which lifted off from New York's Kennedy Airport at 9:35 a.m. under overcast skies on Sunday, Oct. 26, took only nine and a half ~~hours carry~~ Wilmot Glay home to Liberia and away from Providence College forever.

It had taken Wilmot more than a decade of struggling to overcome odds that he described "as a million to one" to reach from the jungle village of Tuscon in Liberia's upcountry to the classrooms of Providence College.

However, his dreamlike story came to a tragic end on Oct. 12 in Rhode Island Hospital. Wilmot, a sophomore, succumbed to complication arising from what doctor's diagnosed as severe aplasic anemia, a rare disease that causes the body to cease producing vital bone marrow.

Wilmot's journey to Providence College began as an 11-year-old third grader when he met Norman Peters, a Peace Corps volunteer who taught school in Tuscon and was virtually adopted by Wilmot's family.

"I recognized Wilmot's potential," Norman Peters recalled, "and I convinced his father — a wise and hard working man — to send Wilmot to a Catholic school in Monrovia, Liberia's capital city." Wilmot continued to perform exceptionally and eventually joined Peters, who had returned to Washington, D.C., in the United States. Upon graduating from Gonzaga High School in Washington he was accepted by Providence and awarded the college's Martin Luther King Scholarship. He majored in business management.

It was not until early this fall that he began to experience any difficulties. He could not keep up during the soccer team sprints. One day he scraped his knee and it would not stop bleeding. Finally he checked into the college's infirmary with a high fever.

After his condition was diagnosed, doctors concluded that the only treatment was a bone marrow transplant from a sibling. A decision was made to fly three members of Wilmot's family from Liberia to Providence. Father Peterson guaranteed payment of all costs. Two Providence College graduates, James A. McKenna '37 and Martin K. Donovan '68, in Senator Pastore's office worked to clear away the red tape in Washington to permit entrance of Lucy, Annie and Alfred Glay. In Monrovia, another P.C. alumnus, Edward J. Carroll '69, third secretary in the American Embassy, made arrangements for visas.

Despite these extraordinary efforts, which the doctors described as "outstanding", Wilmot unexpectedly succumbed the day after his sisters and brother arrived in Providence and before preparations could begin for the bone marrow transplant.

In his brief 22 years on this earth he had overcome obstacles few of us will ever face. His courage, laughter and friendship will not soon be forgotten.

Wilmot Glay [right foreground] watching a Providence soccer game last season with his teammates.

Reprinted from PROVIDENCE Magazine, Winter 1975

23
CHAPTER

TUZON WOMEN.

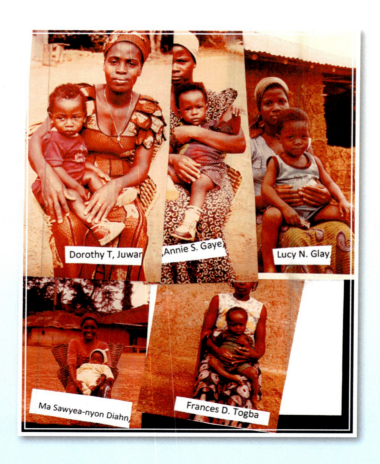

Dorothy T, Juwan

Annie S. Gaye

Lucy N. Glay

Ma Sawyea-nyon Diahn,

Frances D. Togba

Printed in the United States
by Baker & Taylor Publisher Services